Malcolm Leod Mcphail

**Winnowed Anthems for Quartet and Chorus Choirs**

Malcolm Leod McPhail

**Winnowed Anthems for Quartet and Chorus Choirs**

ISBN/EAN: 9783337296704

Printed in Europe, USA, Canada, Australia, Japan

Cover: Foto ©Thomas Meinert / pixelio.de

More available books at **www.hansebooks.com**

# WINNOWED ANTHEMS

FOR

## QUARTET AND CHORUS CHOIRS

EDITED BY

M. L. McPHAIL

NO. I

PUBLISHED BY
THE HOPE PUBLISHING COMPANY
167 WABASH AVENUE
CHICAGO

# Winnowed Anthems.

## VENITE. EXULTEMUS DOMINO.
William Boyce.

PSALM XCV.

1 O COME, let us sing un- | to the | Lord: ‖ let us heartily rejoice in the | strength of | our sal- | vation.
2 Let us come before his presence | with thanks- | giving, ‖ and show ourselves | glad in | him with | psalms.
3 For the Lord is a | great— | God, ‖ and a great | King a- | bove all | gods.
4 In his hands are all the corners | of the | earth: ‖ and the strength of the | hills is | his— | also.
5 The sea is his, | and he | made it: ‖ and his hands pre- | pared the | dry— | land.
6 O come, let us worship | and fall | down. ‖ and kneel be- | fore the | Lord our | Maker.
7 For he is the | Lord our | God, ‖ and we are the people of his pasture, and the | sheep of | his— | hand.
8 O worship the Lord in the | beauty of | holiness; ‖ let the whole earth | stand in | awe of | him.
9 For he cometh, for he cometh to | judge the | earth, ‖ and with righteousness to judge the world, and the | people | with his | truth.

## PRAISE YE THE LORD.
M. L. McPhail.

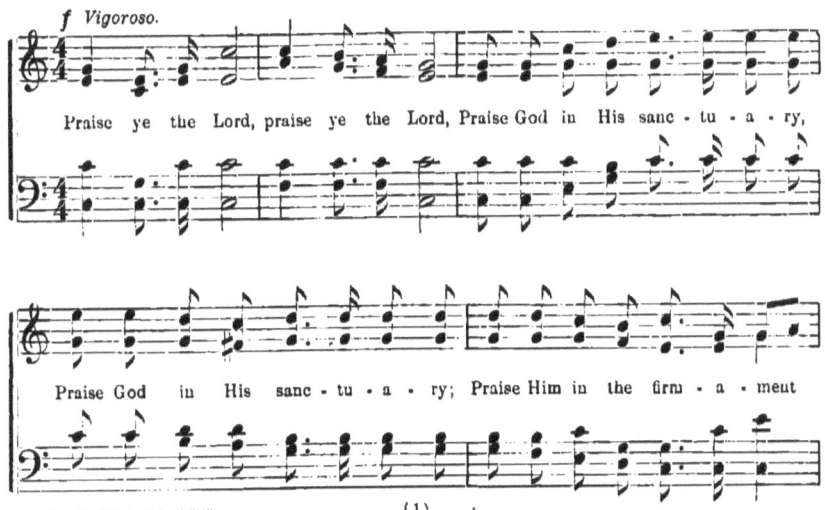

Copyright, 1891, by M. L. McPhail.    (1)

## Praise Ye the Lord.

## Praise Ye the Lord. 3

# TRUST HIM MORE.

W. A. Ogden.

Copyright, 1891, by W. A. Ogden. Used by per.

## Waiting on the Lord.

# Waiting on the Lord.

## THOU, O GOD, ART PRAISED IN SION. 9

Psa. lxv: 1, 8-13.                                                            H. P. Danks.

Used by per. of P. P. Bilhorn, owner of copyright.

## Thou, O God, Art Praised in Sion.

## Thou, O God, Art Praised in Sion.

# COME UNTO ME.

J. V. Henderson.

1. Come un-to me when shadows darkly gath-er, When the sad heart is weary and distressed, Seek-ing for com-fort from your heav'n-ly Fa-ther, Come un-to me, And I will give you rest.

2. Large are the man-sions in thy Fa-ther's dwell-ing, Glad are the homes that sor-rows nev-er dim. Sweet are the harps in

3. There like an E-den blos-som-ing in glad-ness, Bloom the fair flow'rs the earth too rude-ly pressed; Come un-to me, all ye who droop in sad-ness, Come un-to me, And I will give you rest.

Copyright, 1894, by J. P. Vance. By per.

# 16 BEHOLD WHAT MANNER OF LOVE.

M. L. McPhail.

Copyright, 1894, by M. L. McPhail. By per.

## Behold what Manner of Love.

## Jehovah Reigns.

## Jehovah Reigns.

## MAKE A JOYFUL NOISE.

M. L. McPhail.

Copyright, 1895, by M. L. McPhail.

## Make a Joyful Noise.

## 24 Make a Joyful Noise.

## Come Close to the Savior.

## SUN OF MY SOUL.

M. L. McPhail.

Copyright 1894, by M. L. McPhail.

## Sun of my Soul.

## 30 WAKE THE SONG OF JUBILEE.

H. W. Fairbank. By per.

## Wake the Song of Jubilee. 31

ech - o o'er the sea, Loud as might - - - y
Loud as might - y

thun - ders roar, or the ful - ness of the sea, Wake the song of ju - bi -

lee, Let it ech - o o'er the sea, Wake the song of ju - bi -
of ju - - bi - - lee,

lee, Let it ech - o, ech - o o'er the sea, Wake the song of ju - bi -
of ju - - bi - - lee,

lee, Let it ech - o o'er the sea. Loud as might - y, might - y

## Wake the Song of Jubilee.

## O Send Out Thy Light.

## REJOICE AND SING.

Chas. H. Gabriel.

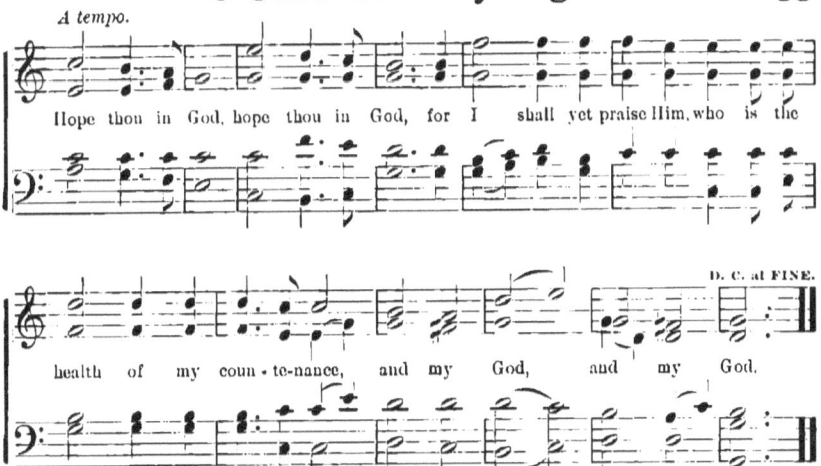

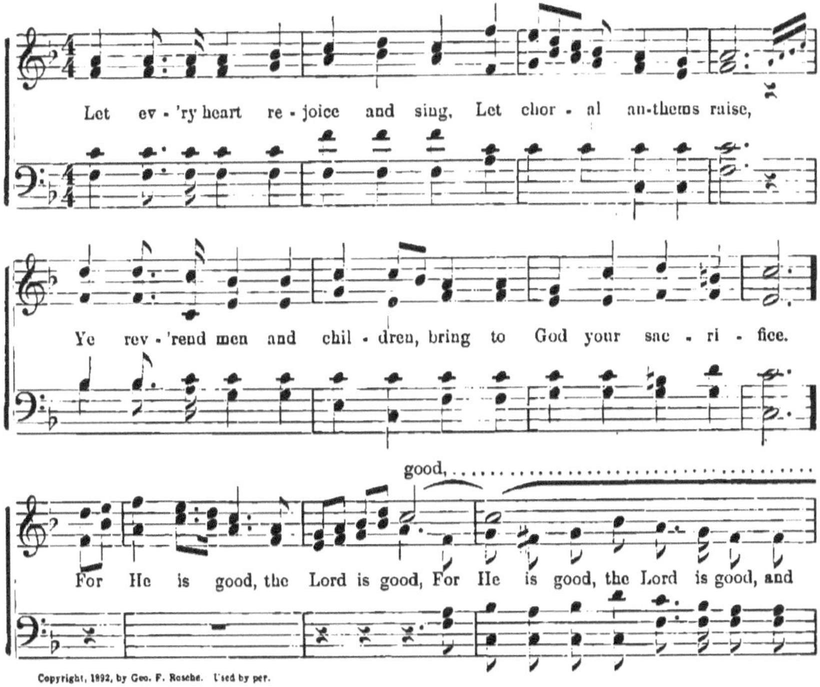

## 36. Rejoice and Sing.

## 38    O LORD, HOW EXCELLENT.
H. R. Palmer.

## O Lord, How Excellent. 39

## O Lord, How Excellent.

## THE PLACE OF PRAYER.

M. L. McPhail.

## The Place of Prayer.

## The Place of Prayer.

# GLORY TO GOD IN THE HIGHEST. 43

From "The Sovereign Choir," by per.

# 44 Glory to God in the Highest.

## Glory to God in the Highest. 45

## The Priceless Pearl. 47

## EVERY HOUR I NEED THY BLESSING.

Elizabeth J. T.  Will L. Thompson.

By permission of Will L. Thompson & Co., East Liverpool, Ohio.

# NEARER, MY GOD, TO THEE. 49

M. L. McPhail.

1. Near - er, my God, to Thee, Near - er my God to Thee! E'en though it
3. Bright doth the truth ap - pear, Shin - ing so clear from heav'n; This light Thou

be a cross that rais - eth me; Still all my song shall be,
send - est me, in mer - cy giv'n; Ev - er to beck - on me,

Near - er, my God, to Thee, Near - er, my God, to Thee, Near - er, to Thee.
Near - er, my God, to Thee, Near - er, my God, to Thee, Near - er, to Thee.

*SOLO. Soprano or Tenor.

Though like a wan - der - er, Day - light all gone, Dark - ness comes o - ver me,
Lord, I would scale the height, Near - er to be, My soul would wing its flight

CHORUS.

Organ.
My rest a stone. Yet e - ven here I'd be Near - er, my
Quick - ly to Thee. Oh! may each day bear me Near - er, my

God, to Thee, Near - er, my God, to Thee, Near - er to Thee.

*Organist will please play the Solo with the right hand.
Copyright, 1894, by M. L. McPhail.

## 50 PRAISE THE NAME OF THE LORD.

Ps. cxlvi.  
Chas. Edw. Pollock.

## Praise the Name of the Lord. 51

## 52. Praise the Name of the Lord.

## Praise the Name of the Lord. 53

## O How Amiable. 55

## 56    O How Amiable.

dwell in Thy house; They will be al - way prais - ing Thee, they will be al - way prais-ing Thee; For they will be al - way prais - ing Thee. Thee.

Bless - ed, bless - ed, bless - ed is the man, bless - ed is the
Bless - ed, bless - ed, bless - ed is the man, bless - ed is the

man whose strength is in Thee; Bless - ed, bless - ed, bless - ed is the
man whose strength is in Thee; Bless - ed, bless - ed, bless - ed is the

man, bless - ed is the man, bless - ed is the man whose strength is in
man, bless - ed is the man, bless - ed is the man whose strength is in

Thee, whose strength is in Thee, whose strength, whose strength is in Thee, A - men.

# THERE WERE SHEPHERDS.

*Not too fast.*            Richard Earle.

There were shep-herds a-bid-ing in the field, (in the field,) Keep-ing watch o'er their flocks by night, (by night,) And the an-gel of the Lord came up-on them, And they were sore a-fraid; And sud-den-ly there was with the an-gels, A mul-ti-tude of the heav'n-ly host, A mul-ti-tude of the heav'n-ly host, Prais-ing God, and say-ing: Glo-ry be to God! and good will tow'rd men! Glo-ry be to God! and good will tow'rd men! Glo - - - - ry be to God!.......... and on earth

From "The Sovereign Choir." By per.

## 58 There were Shepherds.

## There were Shepherds. 59

## Alas! and did my Savior Bleed?

## Praise the Lord.

## 68 Praise the Lord.

## OH! HOW LOVELY IS ZION.

## I'm Nearing the Goal.

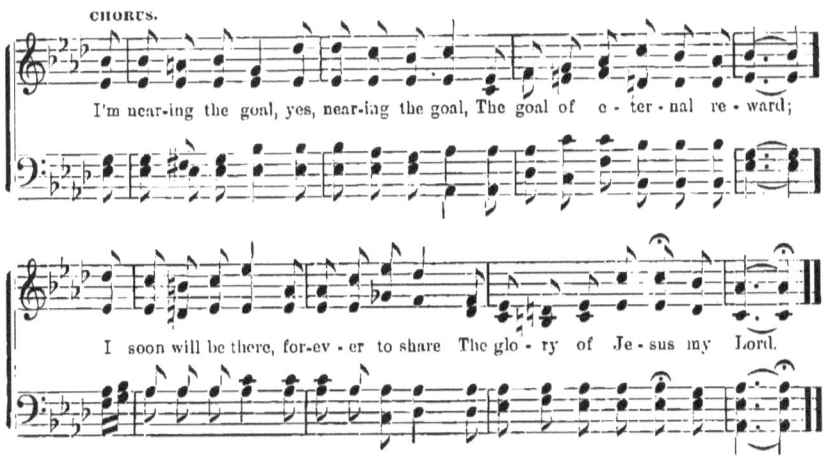

## JESUS, REFUGE OF MY SOUL.

Charles Wesley.     (Hymn Anthem.)     M. L. McPhail.
*Moderato. Con espressione.*

Je - sus, ref - uge of my soul, Let me to Thy bo - som fly,

While the rag - ing bil - lows roll,...... While the tem-pest still is high;

Hide me, O my Sav-ior, hide,
    hide, oh, hide me,
Till the storm of life is past;
    oh, hide me;

Copyright, 1895, by M. L. McPhail.

## 72. Jesus, Refuge of My Soul.

Safe in-to the ha-ven guide, Oh, re-ceive me home at last;
Safe in-to...... the ha-ven guide, Oh, re-ceive me home at last.
Safe in-to the ha-ven guide,

*SOLO. Soprano or Alto.*

Oth-er ref-uge have I none; Hangs my help-less soul on Thee;
Leave, oh, leave me not a-lone! Still sup-port and com-fort me,
Still sup-port and com-fort me.

*CHORUS.*

All my trust on Thee is stayed;

## Jesus, Refuge of My Soul. 73

All my help from Thee I bring; Cover my defenceless head With the shadow of Thy wing.

*SOLO. Soprano or Alto.*

Thou, O Christ, art all I want, All I need in Thee I find;.... Thou didst strengthen me when faint; Now my eyes no more are blind.

*CHORUS.*

Thou of life the fountain art, Rich supplies I find in Thee, Springing up within my heart, Rising to eternity.

*D. C. al FINE.*

## Bless the Lord.

76  Bless the Lord.

## Bless the Lord.

## What are These? 79

# What are These?

# PRAISE UNTO THE FATHER.

Moderato a Molto voce.        A. Beirly.

Copyright, 1894, by W. A. Ogden. Used by permission.

## Praise unto the Father.

## 84. Praise unto the Father.

## Praise unto the Father.

## God of My Salvation. 87

## God of My Salvation. 89

crowned us, Glad to join............ our ho-ly song.
crowned us,

Hal-le-lu-jah, hal-le-lu-jah, hal-le-lu-jah, hal-le-lu-jah!

Love and praise to Christ be-long, Love and praise to Christ be-long,

Love and praise to Christ be-long, Love and praise to Christ be-

long. A-men, A-men, A-men, A-men, A...men.

90 HE SHALL COME DOWN LIKE RAIN.

## He Shall Come Down Like Rain. 91

## 92. He Shall Come Down Like Rain.

sea to sea; and from the riv-er un-to the ends of the earth. earth.

His name shall endure, shall en-dure for-ev-er; His name shall be con-tin-ued, His name shall be con-tin-ued as long as the sun: as long as the sun: and men shall be bless'd in Him: and men shall be bless'd in Him: All nations shall call Him bless-ed. His bless-ed. Bless-ed be the Lord God, the God of Is-ra-el, who on-ly do-eth wondrous things, who on-ly do-eth won-drous things, And

## The Lord is King.

## 96 SOURCE OF LIFE ETERNAL.

*"And this is life eternal, that they might know thee, the only true God, and Jesus Christ, whom thou hast sent."—Jesus.*

G. M. Bills.　　　　　　　　　　　　　　　　　　　　M. L. McPhail.
*Smoothly and not too fast.*

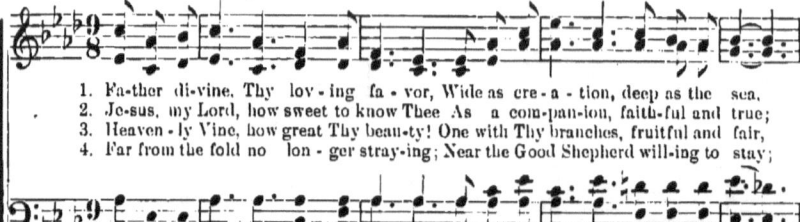

1. Fa-ther di-vine, Thy lov-ing fa-vor, Wide as cre-a-tion, deep as the sea,
2. Je-sus, my Lord, how sweet to know Thee As a com-pan-ion, faith-ful and true;
3. Heaven-ly Vine, how great Thy beau-ty! One with Thy branches, fruitful and fair,
4. Far from the fold no lon-ger stray-ing; Near the Good Shepherd will-ing to stay;

D. C. Cho.—*Un-to the source of life e-ter-nal, Hasteth my soul, O Fa-ther di-vine!*

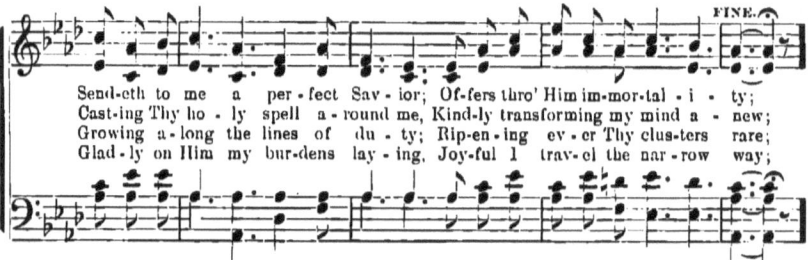

Send-eth to me a per-fect Sav-ior; Of-fers thro' Him im-mor-tal-i-ty;
Cast-ing Thy ho-ly spell a-round me, Kind-ly transforming my mind a-new;
Growing a-long the lines of du-ty; Rip-en-ing ev-er Thy clus-ters rare;
Glad-ly on Him my bur-dens lay-ing, Joy-ful I trav-el the nar-row way;

*Fountain of light and joy su-per-nal, Ev-er up-on me thro' Je-sus shine.*

DUET.

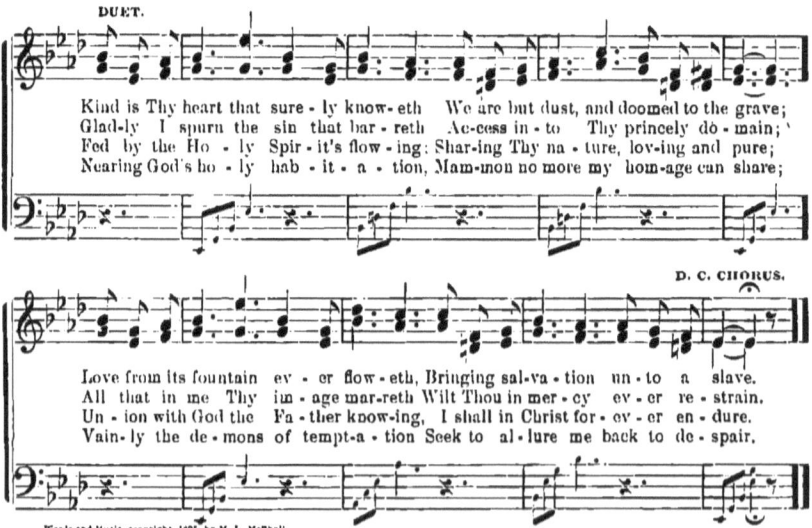

Kind is Thy heart that sure-ly know-eth We are but dust, and doomed to the grave;
Glad-ly I spurn the sin that bar-reth Ac-cess in-to Thy princely do-main;
Fed by the Ho-ly Spir-it's flow-ing; Shar-ing Thy na-ture, lov-ing and pure;
Nearing God's ho-ly hab-it-a-tion, Mam-mon no more my hom-age can share;

D. C. CHORUS.

Love from its fountain ev-er flow-eth, Bringing sal-va-tion un-to a slave.
All that in me Thy im-age mar-reth Wilt Thou in mer-cy ev-er re-strain.
Un-ion with God the Fa-ther know-ing, I shall in Christ for-ev-er en-dure.
Vain-ly the de-mons of tempt-a-tion Seek to al-lure me back to de-spair,

Words and Music, copyright, 1895, by M. L. McPhail.

## The Lord is My Light. 99

## Oh, Give Thanks.

101

Who can ut-ter the might-y acts of the Lord? Who can show forth all His prais-es?

*First time Soprano and Alto Duet.*

Oh, that men would praise the Lord for His good-ness, for His good-ness,
Praise, oh, praise the Lord, praise Him for His good-ness,

Oh, that men would praise the Lord for His wonderful works to the chil-dren of men.
Praise, oh, praise the Lord for His works to the chil-dren of men.

SOLO. Alto.

Let them sac-ri-fice the sac-ri-fic-es of thanks-

giv-ing, And de-clare His works, His works with re-joic-ing.

\* *Small notes for repeat only.*

## Oh, Give Thanks.

## Oh, Give Thanks. 103

Oh, give thanks, oh, give thanks un - to the Lord. A - men. A - men.

## HOLY SPIRIT, FAITHFUL GUIDE.

M. M. Wells.     (Hymn Anthem.)     M. L. McPhail.

*Andante legato, con espressione.*

Ho - ly Spir - it, faith - ful Guide, Ev - er near the Chris-tian's side,

Gen - tly lead us by the hand, Pil-grims in a des - ert land; Wea - ry

souls for aye re - joice, While they hear that sweet-est voice Whisp'ring soft - ly,

FINE.

"Trav-'ler, come; Fol-low me, I'll guide thee home."

Copyright, 1895, by M. L. McPhail.

108 COME, THOU FOUNT.

E. O. Excell.

## Come, Thou Fount.

# Come, Thou Fount.

## Come, Thou Fount.

## Come, Thou Fount.

# GOD SO LOVED THE WORLD. 113

M. L. McPhail.

## God so Loved the World.

# God so Loved the World.

## The Lord will Comfort Zion.

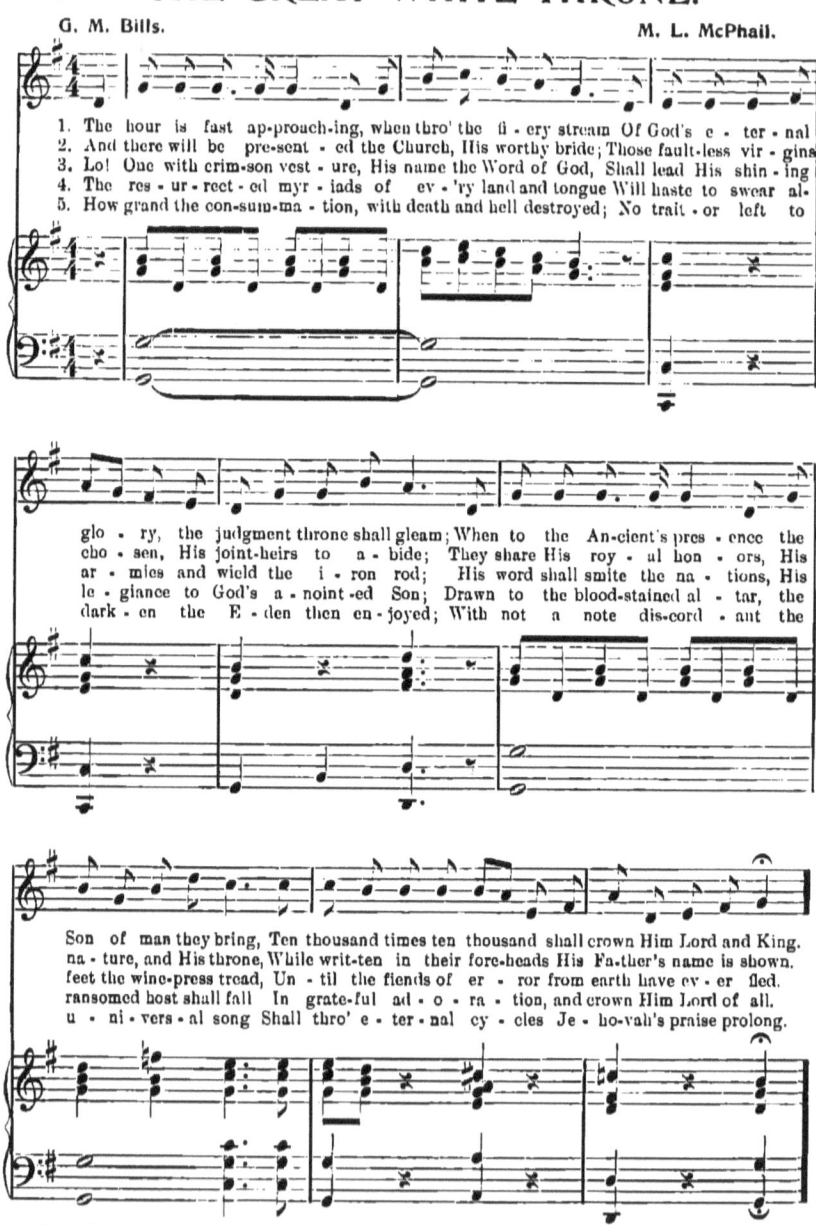

## 120 'Twas in the Watches of the Night.

## 'Twas in the Watches of the Night.

## O Come, Let us Sing.   123

# O Come, Let us Sing.

## O Come, Let us Sing.

## Father Omnipotent.

# THERE AROSE A GREAT STORM. 129

J. B. Herbert.

*p Andante.*

What man-ner of man is this (is this), What man-ner of man is this (is this), That e - ven the winds and the sea, ........ the winds and the sea o - bey Him!

the winds and the sea,

*Agitato.*    *f*

There a-rose a great storm of wind, there a-rose a great storm of wind,

*Cres. - - - - e - - - - -*

And the waves, the waves beat in-to the ship, the waves, the waves beat in-to the ship,

*ff Accel - - - - - - er - - an - - - do.*

There a - rose a great storm, a storm of wind, and the waves, the waves beat in-to the ship.

Copyright, 1893, by Fillmore Bros. Used by per.

## There Arose a Great Storm.

## There Arose a Great Storm. 131

## Praise to Thee. 135

blos - soms by the stream - let, To Thee their beau - ty yield.

*Ad lib.*

**BASS OBLIGATO.** *Sempre staccato.*

Praise, praise to Thee! Praise, praise to Thee! Praise, praise to Thee!

Yes, we............ who know the

Praise, praise to Thee! Praise, praise to Thee! Praise, praise to Thee!

sto - - ry Of Thy............ re-deem-ing love,............ Who

Praise, praise to Thee! Al - might-y Sav - ior, Praise, praise to Thee! our

hope......... to share Thy glo - ry, Thy ris - - - en life a -

ris - en King, Praise, praise to Thee! Praise, praise to Thee!

bove,........ Shall bring............ Thee sweet-er trib - - ute Than

# GLORY BE TO GOD IN THE HIGHEST. 137

(CHRISTMAS ANTHEM.)

Will L. Thompson.

By permission of Will L. Thompson & Co., East Liverpool, Ohio.

138 Glory be to God in the Highest.

## Glory be to God in the Highest. 139

## The Star of Bethlehem.

# The Star of Bethlehem.

## The Star of Bethlehem. 143

## Wake the Song. 147

## 148. Wake the Song.

Wake the Song.

## Sing Praises.

# Sing Praises. 153

*And to sing prais-es, sing prais-es, Sing prais-es un-to Thy name,*
*Sing prais-es, sing prais-es, Sing prais-es un-to Thy name,*

*And to sing prais-es, sing prais-es, Sing prais-es un-to Thy name,*
*Sing prais-es, sing prais-es, Sing prais-es un-to Thy name,*

*O Thou, Most Highest, O Thou, Most High-est, O Thou, Most High . . est.*

## THE LORD IS MY SHEPHERD.

John P. Thomas.

*The Lord is my Shep-herd, I shall not want; He*

*mak-eth me to lie down, to lie down in green pas-tures, And*

Copyright, 1895, by John P. Thomas. Used by per.

## 154 The Lord is My Shepherd.

## 156 CHRIST, THE LORD, IS RISEN TO-DAY.

M. Lindsey.

1. Christ, the Lord, is ris'n to-day, Sons of men and an-gels say;
Raise your joys and tri-umphs high; Sing, ye heav'ns—and earth re-ply.

D. C. 4. Lives a-gain our glo-rious King; Where, O death, is now thy sting?
Once He died, our souls to save; Where's thy vic-t'ry, boast-ing grave?

2. Love's re-deem-ing work is done, Fought the bat-tle, vic-t'ry won; Lo! He's ris-en con-quer-or, And shall

Used by per.

*This Chorus is to be sung after each Solo, or three times altogether. Last time sing the fourth stanza.

## Christ, the Lord, is Risen To=day. 157

## Come, Ye Disconsolate!

# 162 GOD IS THE REFUGE.

John R. Sweney.

Used by per. of John J. Hood, owner of copyright.

## God is the Refuge. 163

Thee, O Lord, do I put my trust, In
God is the ref-uge of His peo-ple, God is the ref-uge of His peo-ple, A
Thee, O Lord, do I put my trust; O let me never be con-
ver-y pres-ent help in trouble, A ver-y present help in trouble;
found-ed, Let me nev-er be con-found-ed;
God is the ref-uge of His peo-ple, A ver-y pres-ent help in
Thou art the ref-uge of Thy peo-ple, There-fore will we nev-er fear.
troub-le, a pres-ent help, There-fore will we nev-er fear.

## 168. ROCKED IN THE CRADLE.

Fred. A. Fillmore.

## Rocked in the Cradle. 169

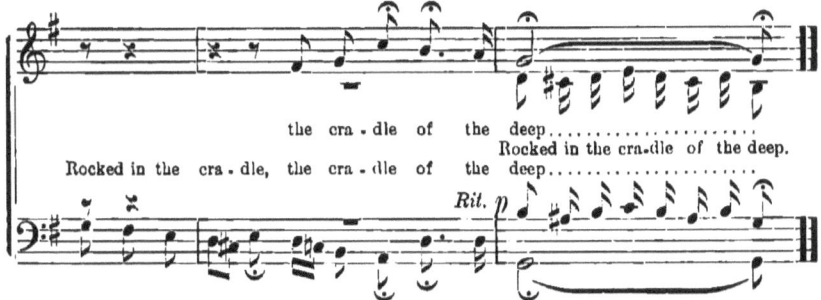

## 172    Christ, Our Passover.

## Christ, Our Passover. 173

172 Christ, Our Passover.

## Christ, Our Passover. 173

## 174. I WILL SING OF THE MERCIES.

J. H. Fillmore.

Used by per. of Fillmore Bros., owners of copyright.

## I Will Sing of the Mercies. 175

# 176. I Will Sing of the Mercies.

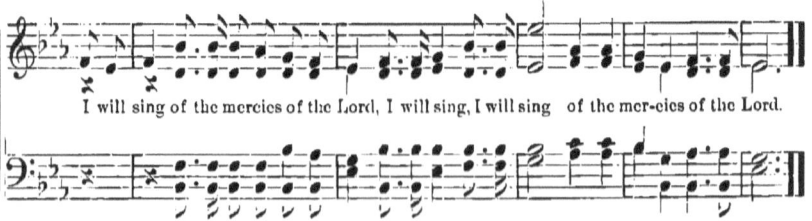

## Jubilee Echoes. 183

# AND THE PUBLICAN.

*Not too fast.*

M. L. McPhail.

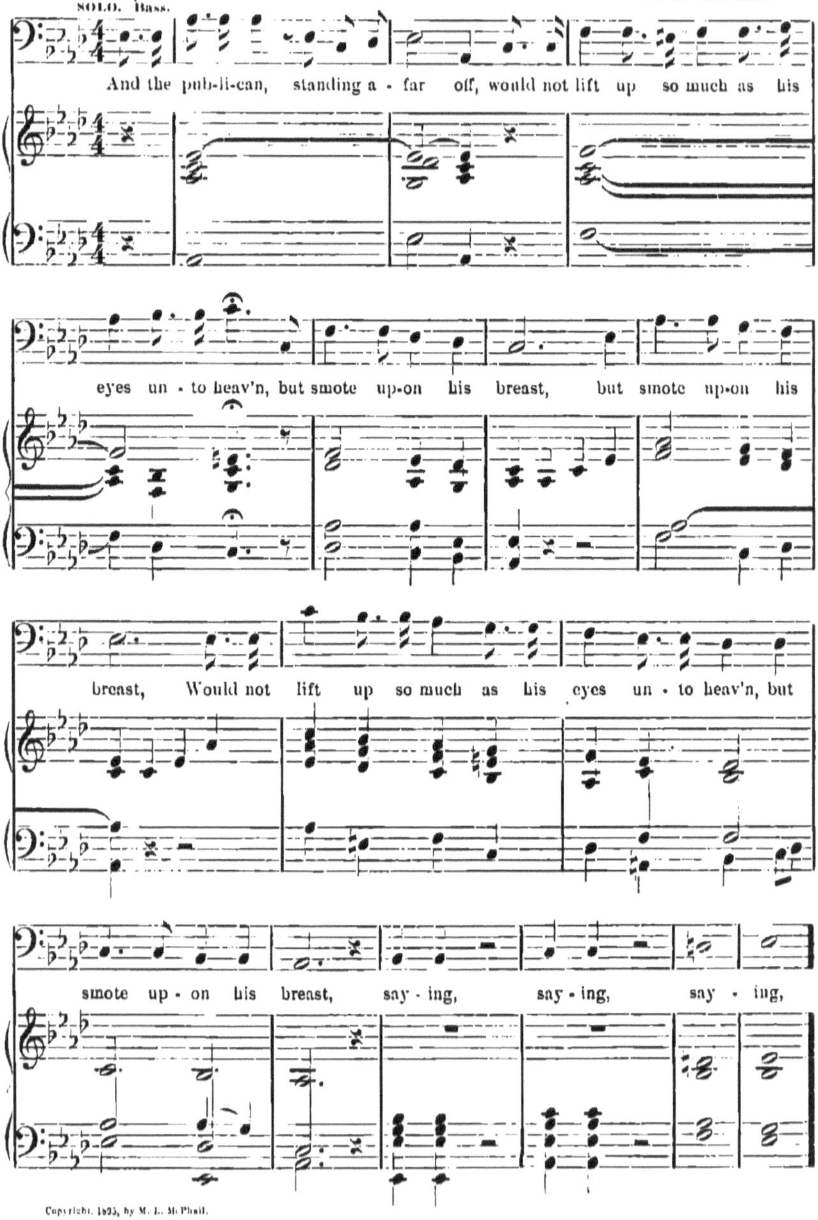

## And the Publican.

# 186 And the Publican.

# INDEX.

| Titles and First Lines. | Writer. | Page. | Titles and First Lines. | Writer. | Page. |
|---|---|---|---|---|---|
| Alas! And did My Savior Bleed | McPhail | 62 | O Lord, Our Lord, How Excellent | Palmer | 38 |
| Always Something | McPhail | 132 | O Come let Us Sing | McPhail | 122 |
| And the Publican | McPhail | 184 | O Come let Us Sing unto the Lord | Emerson | 177 |
| As the Hart | Showalter | 144 | O How Amiable | McPhail | 54 |
| Behold a Stranger at the Door | McClose | 5 | O Lord how Excellent | Palmer | 38 |
| Behold what Manner of Love | McPhail | 16 | O Send out Thy Light | McPhail | 33 |
| Bless the Lord | Tenney | 74 | O Thou God of My Salvation | O'Kane | 86 |
| Christ, Our Passover | McPhail | 170 | Praise the Lord, Praise the Lord | Pollock | 50 |
| Christ, the Lord is Risen To-day | Lindsey | 156 | Praise, Praise, Praise to Thee | Kirkpatrick | 133 |
| Come Close to the Savior | Palmer | 26 | Praise the Name of the Lord | Pollock | 50 |
| Come, Thou Fount | Excell | 108 | Praise to Thee | Kirkpatrick | 133 |
| Come Unto Me | Henderson | 12 | Praise Unto the Father | Beirly | 81 |
| Come, Ye Disconsolate | McPhail | 158 | Praise Waiteth for Thee | Beirly | 81 |
| Crown Him | Buchanan | 13 | Praise Ye the Lord | McPhail | 1 |
| Every Day I'm Nearer Jesus | Lorenz | 164 | Praise Ye the Lord | Lorenz | 60 |
| Every Hour I Need Thy Blessing | Thompson | 47 | Praise the Lord | McPhail | 65 |
| Father Divine, Thy Loving Favor | McPhail | 96 | Praise Ye the Lord | Palmer | 166 |
| Father Omnipotent | Evans | 126 | Rejoice and Sing | Gabriel | 35 |
| For God So Loved the World | McPhail | 113 | Rock of Ages | Showalter | 155 |
| Glory be to God in the Highest | Thompson | 137 | Rock of Ages | Nelson | 180 |
| Glory, Glory, Glory to God | Beirly | 43 | Rocked in the Cradle | Fillmore | 168 |
| Glory to God in the Highest | Beirly | 43 | Sing Praises | Herbert | 150 |
| God is the Refuge | Sweney | 162 | Sing Unto the Lord | Emerson | 177 |
| God of My Salvation | O'Kane | 86 | Since Thy Father's Arm Sustains | Ogden | 4 |
| God So Loved the World | McPhail | 113 | Source of Life Eternal | McPhail | 96 |
| Guide Me, O Thou Great Jehovah | McPhail | 187 | Sun of My Soul | McPhail | 27 |
| Hallelujah, Hallelujah | McPhail | 78 | The Great White Throne | McPhail | 118 |
| He Shall Come Down Like Rain | McPhail | 90 | The Hour is Fast Approaching | McPhail | 118 |
| Holy Spirit, Faithful Guide | McPhail | 103 | The Lord is King | Chapple | 93 |
| Holy Spirit from Above | Palmer | 64 | The Lord is My Light | Prior | 97 |
| How Lovely is Zion | Werschkul | 106 | The Lord is My Shepherd | Thomas | 153 |
| I Come to Thee | McPhail | 15 | The Lord Jehovah Reigns | Beirly | 18 |
| If You Cannot Like the Master | McPhail | 132 | The Lord Will Comfort Zion | Rosencrans | 116 |
| I'm Nearing the Goal | McPhail | 70 | The Place of Prayer | McPhail | 40 |
| It is a Good Thing to Give Thanks | Herbert | 150 | The Priceless Pearl | McPhail | 46 |
| I will Sing of the Mercies | Fillmore | 174 | The Star of Bethlehem | Stillman | 140 |
| Jehovah Reigns | Beirly | 18 | There's a Pearl of Priceless Worth | McPhail | 46 |
| Jesus, Refuge of My Soul | McPhail | 25 | There Arose a Great Storm | Herbert | 129 |
| Jesus, Refuge of My Soul | McPhail | 71 | There were Shepherds | Earle | 57 |
| Jesus, Where'er Thy People Meet | McPhail | 40 | They that Wait Upon the Lord | Gabriel | 6 |
| Jubilee Echoes | McPhail | 182 | Thou, O God, art Praised in Zion | Danks | 9 |
| Knocking at the Door | McClose | 5 | Trust Him More | Ogden | 4 |
| Lead Kindly Light | Palmer | 188 | 'Twas in the Watches of the Night | Nelson | 119 |
| Let Every Heart Rejoice and Sing | Gabriel | 35 | Venite, Exultemus Domino | Boyce | 1 |
| Listen to the Voice Celestial | McPhail | 182 | Waiting on the Lord | Gabriel | 6 |
| Make a Joyful Noise | McPhail | 21 | Wake the Song | McPhail | 145 |
| Nearer Jesus | Lorenz | 164 | Wake the Song of Jubilee | Fairbank | 30 |
| Nearer, My God, to Thee | McPhail | 49 | What are These? | | 78 |
| Oh, Come let Us Sing | Boyce | 1 | What Manner of Man is This? | Herbert | 129 |
| Oh, Give Thanks | Straub | 100 | When Marshaled in the Nightly | Stillman | 140 |
| Oh, How Lovely is Zion | Fairbank | 68 | While on the Broad Road | McPhail | 70 |
| Oh, How Lovely is Zion | Werschkul | 106 | | | |

www.ingramcontent.com/pod-product-compliance
Lightning Source LLC
Chambersburg PA
CBHW032139160426
43197CB00008B/701